Acknowledgement

As we come to the end of this book, "Parenting Teens with PTSD," we are filled with gratitude for the support, encouragement, and inspiration that guided us during this transforming journey. We would like to convey our heartfelt thanks to the individuals and organizations that played a crucial part in making this book a reality.

First and foremost, we extend our heartfelt appreciation to the courageous youngsters who shared their tales, struggles, and victories with us. Your resilience and strength in the face of hardship have been the driving forces behind this book. Your willingness to open your hearts and share your stories will definitely have a great influence on parents, caregivers, and families experiencing similar circumstances.

To the parents and caregivers who navigated the difficulties of PTSD with unflinching love and dedication, we express our heartfelt gratitude. Your devotion to understanding, supporting, and empowering your teenagers is a witness to the tremendous love and concern parents have for their children.

We are immensely thankful to the mental health specialists and experts who freely donated their knowledge and views, improving the content of this book. Your experience has been crucial in providing accurate and helpful information to our readers.

To our friends and family members who provided constant support and encouragement during this journey, thank you for being our pillars of strength. Your belief in us and in the value of this book motivated our commitment to make a positive difference in the lives of youth and families affected by PTSD.

A special thank you goes to our publishers, editors, and the entire publishing team, whose devotion and hard work brought this book to reality. Your suggestions and experience have been important in molding this book into its final shape.

Last but not least, we convey our gratitude to our readers. We hope this book has provided you with the insight, support, and skills to empower your teen's journey to healing and recovery.

In conclusion, this book is a testimonial to the power of compassion, empathy, and support in the lives of teenagers and their families. Together, we can build a world where every teen with PTSD feels understood, supported, and motivated to embrace their resilience and go on a path of recovery and optimism.

Table of contents

Chapter 1 : INTRODUCTION

Chapter 2 : Understanding PTSD

Chapter 3 Symptoms of PTSD

Chapter 4 Effects of PTSD in teenagers

Chapter 5. How PTSD Symptoms in teenagers differs from adults

Chapter 6 How trauma can manifest in behaviors, emotions and physical health of teenagers

Chapter 7 Communication techniques to connect with teens with PTSD

Chapter 8 Significance of creating safe and non judgemental feelings and experience with PTSD teens

Chapter 9. Coping mechanisms for parents

Chapter 10. Building resilience with PTSD teens

Chapter 11 Activities to boost PTSD teen's self esteem and emotional strength

Chapter 12. Impacts of PTSD in teens academic performance

Chapter 13. Impacts of PTSD in relationships with family, friends and romantic partners

Chapter 14 Ways to empower PTSD teens to take control of their recovery

Conclusion

Chapter 1

INTRODUCTION

Parenting is a journey filled with joy, hardships, and moments of pride. As parents, we seek to offer our children love, support, and direction, helping them negotiate the complexity of life. However, when our teens encounter the severe impact of Post-Traumatic Stress Disorder (PTSD), the parenting landscape takes on new dimensions that demand knowledge, sensitivity, and a distinct set of abilities.

Welcome to "Parenting Teens with PTSD,"
a book aimed at shedding light on the experiences of parents and caregivers helping adolescents who

are coping with the repercussions of trauma. We know that parenting a teen with PTSD may be an exhausting and sometimes isolated experience. As parents ourselves, we understand the weight of the responsibility and the desire to do everything necessary to help our children heal and grow.

In this book, we begin on a voyage of investigation, looking into the issues faced by both youth and their caregivers as they navigate the complexity of PTSD. We want to provide thorough knowledge of the impact of PTSD on teenagers by studying how it impacts their emotions, behaviors, academic performance, and relationships with family, friends, and romantic partners.

Understanding the unique experiences of kids with PTSD is crucial to creating a safe and supportive place for them to express their feelings and experiences. We emphasize the value of providing a non-judgmental place, enabling open communication, and supporting youth to take ownership of their recovery journey.

Throughout the pages of this book, we will empower parents and caregivers with practical tools and coping skills to accompany their teens through the healing process. We underscore the significance of equipping youth with knowledge, resilience, and a sense of autonomy as they navigate their route to recovery.

Our purpose is to bridge the gap between the issues of PTSD and effective parenting by offering insights, understanding, and assistance for parents and caregivers. By establishing a compassionate and knowledgeable approach, we may empower both youth and their families to negotiate the intricacies of PTSD with strength, resilience, and optimism.

In "Parenting Teens with PTSD," we urge you to go on this transforming journey alongside us. Together, let us discover the power of unconditional love and compassionate understanding and the enormous influence they may have on the lives of youth recovering from trauma. May this book serve as a source of inspiration, empowerment, and support for any parent or caregiver who tries to offer the best possible care for their teen with PTSD.

Chapter 2

Understanding PTSD

A complicated and sometimes crippling mental health disease known as post-traumatic stress disorder (PTSD) can develop in people who have gone through or witnessed a terrible event. Its symptoms can be extremely upsetting and disruptive to daily life, and it can affect people of diverse ages, genders, and backgrounds. It is a psychiatric condition that arises as a result of having experienced, seen, or been exposed to a traumatic incident or sequence. These occurrences frequently pose a threat to life, result in severe injury, or inspire great fear, helplessness, or horror.

Causes of PTSD

A terrible event that you have either experienced or witnessed might lead to post-traumatic stress disorder (PTSD). Not everyone who experiences trauma will get PTSD, although certain circumstances can make it more likely. There are numerous potential causes of PTSD, some of which include:

Experiencing Trauma: Exposure to a traumatic experience is the main cause of post-traumatic stress disorder (PTSD). An incident that involves real or threatened death, significant injury, or sexual violence is referred to as a traumatic event. Natural catastrophes, accidents, physical or sexual assault, military combat, terrorist attacks, and major medical issues are a few examples of traumatic events that can cause PTSD.

Traumatic Event Intensity and Severity: The traumatic event's intensity and severity may have an impact on a person's probability of getting PTSD. More serious or life-threatening traumas may have a bigger effect on a person's psychological health.

Childhood trauma: Childhood trauma, including abuse, neglect, or exposure to domestic violence, dramatically raises the chance of developing post-traumatic stress disorder (PTSD) in adulthood.Previous

Trauma History: Because past traumas can amplify the effects of a current traumatic event, those who have encountered several traumatic events in their lives may be more prone to developing PTSD.

Personal Vulnerability: Some personal characteristics can make someone more susceptible to PTSD. A history of mental health problems, such as anxiety or depression, as well as a family history of mental illness, may fall under this category.

Biological variables: According to some research, PTSD development may be influenced by a variety of biological variables, including genetic susceptibility and neurobiological variations in stress response.

Lack of Social Support: Having a solid support system can help prevent PTSD. On the other hand, people who don't have access to resources or much social support may be more likely to acquire the illness.

Coping strategies: The effectiveness of coping strategies for acute stress can affect the likelihood of acquiring PTSD. People who have trouble coping or who use unhealthy coping techniques may be more vulnerable.

Perceived Lack of Control: During the traumatic experience, a sense of helplessness or lack of control may have contributed to the development of PTSD.

Factors of gender and culture: According to research, PTSD risk may vary depending on factors of gender and culture. For instance, women may be more prone to developing PTSD after experiencing sexual assault, and cultural considerations might influence how trauma is felt and conveyed. It's crucial to remember that the onset of PTSD is the result of a complicated interaction of several circumstances, and personal experiences can differ greatly.

After experiencing a traumatic experience, reaching out for support and professional assistance can be vital to managing the after effects of trauma and lowering the risk of developing PTSD. In order to promote healing and recovery for those who do acquire PTSD, early intervention and adequate therapy are also crucial.

Chapter 3

Symptoms of PTSD

A person's daily life and general well-being can be greatly impacted by a variety of severe and enduring symptoms that are associated with post-traumatic stress disorder (PTSD). These signs usually appear after going through or seeing a distressing experience. Four primary clusters can be used to broadly classify PTSD symptoms:

1. **Having the same symptoms again:**

a. Recurrent, unwanted, and upsetting memories of the traumatic incident are referred to as intrusive memories. These memories could be brought back by certain triggers or reminders of the experience.

b. Flashbacks: The sensation that the terrible event is happening once more or that the person is reliving it right now.

c. Nightmares: Repeated, upsetting dreams that are connected to the traumatic incident extreme physical or psychological

d. Reactions to Reminders: Emotional or physical responses, such as perspiration, heart palpitations, or panic attacks, occur when one is exposed to circumstances, persons, or locations that trigger memories of the trauma.

2. Avoidance Signs and Symptoms

i. Avoiding Trauma-Related Triggers: Consistent attempts to steer clear of ideas, sentiments, words, situations, activities, or individuals connected to the traumatic incident

ii. Emotional Numbing: A feeling of emotional detachment or the inability to feel good feelings

iii. Avoiding Talking About the Trauma: Difficulty or unwillingness to Talk About the Traumatic Event, Despite Encouragement

3. **Mood symptoms and negative thoughts:**

1. Negative Beliefs and Thoughts: Persistent and misguided notions about oneself or others, such as feelings of shame, remorse, or blame stemming from the trauma.

2. Memory Issues: Trouble remembering specific details of the stressful experience.

3. Reduced Interest: Loss of enthusiasm for or absence from previously favorite activities.

4. Emotional Detachment: Feeling emotionally distant from others and finding it difficult to forge or uphold close relationships.

5. Difficulty Feeling Positive Emotions: The inability to feel good feelings, which results in emotional numbness

4. **Reactivity and Arousal Signs:**

a. Hypervigilance: being constantly on the lookout for danger and being unduly vigilant.

b. Anger and Irritability: Regular displays of anger, irritability, or violent behavior.

c. Concentration Issues: Memory, Focus, and Attention Issues.

Chapter 4

Effects of PTSD in teenagers

Teenagers who suffer from post-traumatic stress disorder (PTSD) may experience considerable effects on their emotional, psychological, social, and intellectual performance. The teenage years are already a time of rapid growth and development, and having PTSD might worsen their general state of health.

Teenagers may experience the following effects:

Teenagers with PTSD may have strong, debilitating emotions in relation to their terrible events. They could struggle with emotional regulation, frequent mood changes, and increased irritation.

Teenagers with PTSD may engage in avoidance strategies to deal with upsetting memories or reminders of the experience. Avoiding locations, persons, or activities connected to the traumatic incident may fall under this category.

Academic Difficulties: Teenagers with PTSD may find it difficult to focus and pay attention in class. As a result, they might do worse academically, which could result in lower grades and even learning issues.

Teenagers with PTSD may withdraw from friends and family and from social situations in general. To stay away from triggers or feelings of vulnerability, they could isolate themselves.

Sleep Issues: PTSD can interfere with a teen's sleep cycles and cause sleeplessness, nightmares, or frequent nighttime awakenings. Their emotional turbulence and daily exhaustion may be further exacerbated by sleep difficulties.

Teenagers with PTSD may suffer feelings of helplessness or despair, which might raise their risk of self-harm or suicide thoughts.

Substance addiction: Some youth may turn to alcohol or drugs in an effort to manage their symptoms, which can result in problems with substance addiction.

Teenagers with PTSD may have trouble trusting others because they worry about appearing weak or being betrayed.

Relationship Impact: PTSD can cause tension in friendships, family, and romantic partnerships. Conflicts and misunderstandings may result from PTSD's emotional instability and communication problems.

Negative Self-Image: Teenagers with PTSD may come to blame themselves for the terrible incident or develop negative beliefs about who they are.

Physical Symptoms: Some youth may feel physical signs of psychological anguish, such as headaches, stomachaches, or other unexplained ailments.

Performance in Extracurricular Activities: Teenagers with PTSD may stop participating in hobbies, athletics, or other extracurricular activities that they once found enjoyable.

Secondary Trauma Exposure: Families and caregivers of adolescents with PTSD may also go through secondary trauma, which can have an adverse effect on their own mental health and wellbeing.

Parents, caregivers, and educators must keep an eye out for symptoms of PTSD in teenagers and seek professional assistance when necessary. Teens who are dealing with PTSD might greatly benefit from early intervention and appropriate treatment, such as therapy and support. Many kids can recover and enjoy happy lives if they are given the correct support and resources.

Chapter 5

How PTSD Symptoms in teenagers differs from adults

While the underlying symptoms of PTSD are largely identical between teenagers and adults, there can be some changes in how these symptoms appear in teenagers.

Here are some signs of PTSD in teenagers that may be different from those in adults:

Behavioral Regression: Teens with PTSD may demonstrate regressive behaviors, reverting to behaviors typical of a younger age. This relapse could include bed wetting, thumb sucking, or clinging to parents or caretakers.

Avoidance Through School Avoidance: While adults may avoid places or situations that evoke traumatic memories, teenagers could avoid attending school completely if the traumatic incident or reminders are related to the school environment.

Irritability and Aggression: Adolescents may express their emotions through irritability, furious outbursts, or aggressive behaviors, whereas adults could exhibit more internalized or withdrawn responses.

Recklessness and Self-Destructive Behavior: Some youth may engage in dangerous or self-destructive behaviors as a way to cope with their PTSD symptoms, which may be different from how adults generally cope.

Emotional Dysregulation: Teens may suffer more acute and frequent mood swings compared to adults with PTSD, making it challenging for them to manage their emotions properly.

Social Withdrawal: While both adults and teens could withdraw from social situations, teenagers may withdraw from friends and family more suddenly, resulting in a rapid change in their social behavior.

Externalizing Symptoms: Adolescents may externalize their PTSD symptoms by acting out or participating in troublesome activities, whereas adults could internalize their discomfort more frequently.

Somatic Complaints: Some youth may communicate their mental discomfort through bodily complaints such as headaches, stomachaches, or other inexplicable physical ailments.

Peer Relationships: PTSD can influence peer relationships in teenagers, leading to difficulties in making and keeping friendships and increasing confrontation with peers.

Academic Performance: PTSD can have a substantial influence on a teenager's ability to concentrate, focus, and perform intellectually, which can lead to deteriorating school performance.

It's crucial to be aware of these potential distinctions while screening and supporting an adolescent with PTSD. Early detection and assistance, including professional counseling or therapy, can be critical in helping teenagers manage and recover from PTSD effectively. If you feel a teenager is having PTSD symptoms, receiving expert support from a mental health specialist who specializes in working with teenagers can make a major difference in their rehabilitation.

Chapter 6

How trauma can manifest in behaviors, emotions and physical health of teenagers

Trauma can have enormous consequences for youth, appearing in numerous ways across their behaviors, emotions, and physical health. It's crucial to recognize these manifestations to provide proper assistance and intervention. Here are some common ways trauma might affect teenagers:

BEHAVIORAL MANIFESTATIONS:

a. **Withdrawal**: Trauma can cause youth to withdraw socially, avoiding connections with friends, relatives, or activities they formerly enjoyed.

b. **Aggression**: Some teenagers may exhibit aggressive behaviors as a way to cope with feelings of helplessness or to protect themselves.

c. **Risky Behavior:** Teens may engage in reckless or impulsive acts, seeking stimulation or trying to escape their emotional suffering.

d. **Avoidance**: Teens may avoid events, places, or people that evoke traumatic memories or reminders of the traumatic experience.

f. **School Problems**: Traumatized teenagers may suffer academically, experiencing difficulty with concentration, memory, and focus.

EMOTIONAL MANIFESTATIONS:

a. **Anxiety**: Teens may suffer heightened anxiety, panic attacks, or excessive worry about their safety or the safety of loved ones.

b. **Depression**: Trauma can lead to emotions of sadness, hopelessness, and loss of interest in activities that were once enjoyable.

c. **Guilt and Shame**: Adolescents may blame themselves for the distressing experience or feel ashamed of their reactions to it.

d. **Wrath**: Trauma can generate intense feelings of wrath and impatience, leading to disputes with friends, family members, or authority figures.

e. **Emotional Numbing**: Some teenagers may emotionally detach from others, feeling emotional numbness as a protective mechanism.

Physical Health Manifestations:

a. **Sleep Disturbances:** Trauma can alter sleep patterns, leading to sleeplessness, nightmares, or night terrors.

b. **Chronic weariness**: Teens may feel persistent weariness due to the emotional toll of trauma and sleep difficulties.

c. **Physical Pain**: Trauma can show up in physical symptoms such as headaches, stomachaches, muscle tension, or other unexplained sensations.

d. **Weakened Immune System**: Chronic stress from trauma can weaken the immune system, making youngsters more susceptible to infections.

It's crucial to approach teenagers with empathy, compassion, and patience if they've endured trauma. Encouraging open communication, creating a safe and supportive atmosphere, and obtaining expert help from mental health specialists can substantially benefit their rehabilitation process. Trauma-focused therapies, such as cognitive-behavioral therapy (CBT) or eye movement desensitization and reprocessing (EMDR), are helpful ways for helping youth understand their traumatic experiences and heal from the related emotional and physical consequences.

Chapter 7

Communication techniques to connect with teens with PTSD

Connecting with a teenager who has PTSD demands unique care and thought. Here are some helpful communication approaches for parents to establish a loving and understanding relationship with their PTSD-affected teens:

Educate Yourself: Learn about PTSD and its effects on teenagers to better comprehend your child's experiences. Empathy and expertise will help you approach conversations with sensitivity and compassion.

Be Patient and understanding. Trauma healing is a gradual process, and your kid could have good days and bad days. Be patient with their improvement and offer continuous support throughout their trip.

Create a Safe Environment: Ensure your home is a safe and loving atmosphere where your teen feels secure enough to open up about their feelings and experiences.

Validate Their sentiments: Let your kid know that their sentiments are valid and that you understand they are going through a tough moment. Avoid rejecting or underestimating their emotions.

Use Non-Verbal Communication: Sometimes, verbal communication might be challenging for kids with PTSD. Use non-verbal indicators like hugs, a reassuring touch, or a soft nod to indicate your support and concern.

Practice Active Listening: Listen intently to your teen when they want to talk. Avoid interrupting, and let them express themselves fully. This implies that you respect their views and emotions.

Offer a Sense of Control: Trauma can leave people feeling powerless. Allow your kid to have a say in their treatment plan, therapy alternatives, or daily activities to recover a sense of control in their lives.

Respect boundaries. Understand that your teen might need space at times. Respect their boundaries, and let them know you are there when they are ready to chat.

Use Open-Ended Questions: Ask open-ended questions to enable your teen to express their experiences and emotions more freely. Enable deeper conversations.

Share Information Gently: If you need to discuss difficult themes or family concerns, approach them gently and with respect, noting the potential triggers for your teen.

Mind Your Tone: Pay attention to your tone of voice since it can affect how your teen receives your communication.

Avoid Blame and Guilt: Refrain from blaming or making your teen feel guilty for their experience or any related actions. Focus on supporting them and helping them heal.

Encourage Coping methods: Work together to identify healthy coping methods that help them manage their PTSD symptoms effectively.

Attend Therapy Together: If your teen is in therapy, attend a few sessions together to better understand their progress and obstacles. It can also show your devotion to their well-being.

Applaud Progress: Acknowledge and applaud every small step your teen takes in their healing path. Positive reinforcement may be immensely motivating.

Remember that every teenager's experience with PTSD is unique, and the communication approaches that work best may differ. Stay open, compassionate, and flexible to your teen's needs and preferences, and always be willing to seek expert help to accompany them on their path to healing.

Chapter 8

Significance of creating safe and non judgemental feelings and experience with PTSD teens

Creating safe and non-judgmental venues for sharing feelings and experiences with PTSD teens is of fundamental importance for their well-being and healing. Here are the key benefits of establishing such a supportive atmosphere:

Trauma Processing: A secure and non-judgmental setting helps PTSD kids process their traumatic experiences without fear of judgment or dismissal. Sharing their feelings and experiences honestly can aid in understanding and coping with their trauma.

Emotional Regulation: PTSD teens typically struggle with emotional regulation. By creating a safe setting, kids can express their emotions without feeling overwhelmed or criticized, leading to greater emotional regulation.

Trust Building: Trust is vital for teens with PTSD, as tragedy can shatter their sense of security. A non-judgmental setting creates trust between them and their caregivers, promoting a strong therapeutic connection.

Strengthening Communication: Teens with PTSD could find it tough to communicate their emotions. A non-judgmental setting stimulates open communication, allowing them to express themselves and feel heard.

Reducing Isolation: PTSD can contribute to feelings of isolation and detachment. Creating a safe space develops a sense of belonging and helps kids realize they are not alone in their challenges.

Empowerment and Autonomy: A non-judgmental environment encourages PTSD kids to make decisions about their rehabilitation. When individuals feel heard and valued, they are more inclined to actively participate in their treatment and recovery processes.

Coping techniques: Sharing experiences and feelings might help kids learn healthier coping techniques. A non-judgmental setting encourages discovering positive strategies to manage stress and anxiety.

Reducing Shame and Guilt: Teens with PTSD may blame themselves for their trauma or its effects. A comfortable environment devoid of criticism can lessen feelings of shame and guilt, encouraging self-compassion.

Promoting Resilience: A non-judgmental atmosphere aids in the development of resilience in PTSD youth. Feeling encouraged in their journey towards healing helps promote strength and flexibility.

Encouraging Professional Help: In a safe and non-judgmental atmosphere, teens may feel more comfortable addressing their issues, which can inspire them to seek professional help and support.

Facilitating Family Support: A supportive setting encourages family members to appreciate the problems encountered by their PTSD kid better. This knowledge fosters family support and togetherness in the healing process.

Reducing Triggers: By being non-judgmental, caregivers can prevent unwittingly generating unpleasant feelings or behaviors in the PTSD teen. This helps create a calmer and more stable environment.

Promoting Self-Reflection: A safe and non-judgmental space facilitates self-reflection in PTSD teens. It allows people to explore their thoughts and feelings, leading to greater self-awareness and personal growth.

Long-term Healing: A supportive setting produces a pleasant and healing atmosphere, which can have lasting impacts on a PTSD teen's rehabilitation and general well-being.

Overall, maintaining a safe and non-judgmental atmosphere is crucial for the mental, emotional, and social healing of PTSD teens. It provides the framework for trust, growth, and healing, enabling individuals to manage the challenges of PTSD with increased resilience and hope for the future.

Chapter 9

Coping mechanisms for parents

Parenting teens with PTSD involves particular coping techniques to provide appropriate support and understanding. Here are some coping strategies for parents to traverse this tough journey:

Educate Yourself: Learn about PTSD, its symptoms, and its influence on youth. Understanding the condition will help you respond to your teen's needs more effectively.

Practice Self-Care: Caring for a teen with PTSD can be emotionally draining. Prioritize your own self-care, including regular breaks, relaxation, exercise, and seeking support from friends or support groups.

Seek Professional Help: Engage with mental health professionals who specialize in working with kids with PTSD. They can provide vital guidance and assistance to both you and your teen.

Practice Patience: Be patient with your teen's improvement. Healing from trauma is a lengthy process, and it may take time for your teen to open up and make gains in healing.

Communicate Openly: Maintain open communication with your teen. Let them know they can talk to you about anything without fear of judgment.

Use Active Listening: Practice active listening to understand your teen's feelings and experiences better. Show empathy and validate their emotions.

Set Realistic Expectations: Be realistic about your teen's strengths and limitations. Avoid putting unnecessary pressure on them during their rehabilitation.

Establish Routines: Creating a regulated and predictable atmosphere can help your teen feel safe and comfortable. Consistent routines can provide stability during challenging circumstances.

Be flexible and adaptive in your approach to parenting. Different situations may require different solutions, so be open to altering your parenting approach as needed.

Foster Independence: Encourage your teen's independence while offering a safety net. Allow children to make age-appropriate decisions and take on responsibilities to increase their confidence.

Use Positive Reinforcement: Acknowledge and reward your teen's efforts and achievements, no matter how minor. Positive reinforcement can motivate them to continue their growth.

Teach Coping Skills: Help your teen build healthy coping techniques to manage stress and anxiety. Encourage activities such as journaling, mindfulness, or engaging in hobbies they enjoy.

Practice mindfulness together to help your teen stay present and handle overwhelming emotions.

Engage in Family Activities: Participate in activities that encourage bonding and positive experiences as a family. This might provide a sense of belonging and support.

Advocate for Your Teen: Be your teen's advocate, especially at school or other places where they may need more help or accommodations.

Practice Self-Reflection: Take time to reflect on your parenting method and emotions. Seek support or counseling if needed to process your feelings and reactions.

Be Understanding of Setbacks: Recognize that setbacks are a natural part of the rehabilitation process. Respond to setbacks with patience and support.

Remember that every teen's experience with PTSD is unique, so customize these coping methods to meet your teen's individual requirements and preferences. Prioritizing your own well-being and receiving professional care when necessary can enable you to be a more effective and supportive parent for your teen with PTSD.

Chapter 10

Building resilience with PTSD teens

Building resilience in PTSD kids is vital for helping them cope with their trauma and handle life's challenges more effectively. Resilience is the ability to bounce back from hardship and retain positive mental health despite tough situations. Here are some techniques to develop resilience in kids with PTSD:

Foster a Supportive atmosphere: Create a safe, loving, and supportive home atmosphere where your teen feels accepted and understood. Having a solid support system is vital for growing resilience.

Encourage Open Communication: Encourage your teen to share honestly about their feelings and experiences. Be an engaged and empathic listener, allowing people to express themselves without judgment.

Provide Validation: Validate your teen's emotions and experiences, letting them know that their feelings are valid and accepted. This validation helps boost their emotional well-being and self-esteem.

Promote good Coping Mechanisms: Teach and model good coping methods to your teen. These may include mindfulness, deep breathing exercises, physical activity, creative expression, or indulging in hobbies.

Set Realistic Goals: Encourage your teen to set realistic and achievable goals. Celebrate their growth and victories, no matter how minor, to improve their confidence and motivation.

Focus on Strengths: Help your teen recognize their strengths and talents. Building on these strengths can empower them and remind them of their perseverance.

Teach Problem-Solving Skills: Teach your teen problem-solving skills to help them tackle obstacles effectively. Encourage them to brainstorm solutions and assess potential results.

Promote Social Connections: Encourage positive social interactions and help your teen maintain healthy ties with friends and family members.

Provide Structure and schedule: Establish a regular and predictable daily schedule, as this can provide stability and lessen anxiety for teens with PTSD.

Encourage Help-getting: Educate your teen on the necessity of getting help when required. Encourage them to talk to a mental health professional or a trustworthy adult if they are struggling.

Promote Self-Reflection: Encourage your teen to engage in self-reflection and self-awareness. Understanding their emotions and mental patterns might help individuals better manage their reactions to triggers.

Celebrate perseverance. Acknowledge and celebrate your teen's perseverance and capacity to overcome adversities. Recognize their efforts in managing PTSD and handling difficult situations.

Be a Role Model: Model resilience in your own life by displaying good coping skills, adaptability, and a positive attitude in the face of adversity.

Provide Opportunities for Growth: Encourage your teen to take on new tasks and explore their hobbies. Providing opportunities for growth can boost their confidence and resilience.

Foster a Sense of Purpose: Help your teen identify their passions and interests. Having a sense of purpose and direction helps children continue through difficult circumstances.

Building resilience in PTSD kids is a lengthy process that involves patience, empathy, and continual care. By providing a supportive environment and teaching useful coping skills, you may encourage your teen to tackle their trauma and future problems with strength and resilience. If needed, obtaining professional treatment from a therapist or counselor might further support their resilience-building journey.

Chapter 11

Activities to boost PTSD teen's self esteem and emotional strength

Boosting self-esteem and emotional strength in PTSD teens entails engaging in activities that generate a sense of success, self-awareness, and good emotional experiences.

Creative Expression: Encourage your teen to engage in creative pursuits such as art, writing, music, or dance. Creative expression can provide a healthy outlet for emotions and foster self-discovery.

Physical Exercise: Regular physical activity, such as running, yoga, or team sports, can enhance mood, reduce stress, and boost self-confidence via a sense of achievement.

Mindfulness and Meditation: Practice mindfulness and meditation together to help your teen stay present and handle overwhelming emotions. These practices can build emotional resilience and self-awareness.

Journaling: Encourage your teen to keep a journal to communicate their thoughts and feelings. Writing can be a therapeutic technique to process emotions and obtain insights into one's experiences.

Volunteering: Engaging in community service or volunteering can bring a sense of purpose and success while developing connections with others.

Learning New talents: Encourage your teen to learn new talents or pursue interests they are passionate about. Mastering a new skill can enhance confidence and self-esteem.

Positive Affirmations: Encourage your teen to practice positive self-talk and use daily affirmations to strengthen their sense of self-worth.

Support Groups: Consider linking your teen with support groups where they may interact with peers who have similar experiences. Sharing stories and offering support can improve emotional strength.

Goal Setting: Help your teen develop realistic goals and work towards achieving them. Celebrate their growth and triumphs to support their self-belief.

Outdoor Activities: Spend time in nature with your teen, such as hiking, camping, or gardening. Nature can have a relaxing impact and enhance overall well-being.

Pet Therapy: If possible, consider engaging pets in your teen's daily life. Spending time with animals has been demonstrated to relieve stress and increase emotional well-being.

Positive Role Models: Expose your teen to positive role models, either through literature, movies, or real-life mentors. Seeing others overcome problems might encourage resilience.

Limiting Negative material: Be cautious of the material your teen consumes. Limit exposure to unpleasant or triggering content that may impair their emotional well-being.

Practicing thankfulness: Encourage your teen to focus on the positive elements of their life and express thankfulness for what they have. Gratitude activities can boost general perspective and emotional strength.

Building Healthy Relationships: Support your teen in building healthy and supportive relationships with peers and family members. Positive connections can increase their emotional well-being.

Remember that each teenager is unique, and not all activities will resonate with every individual. It's crucial to listen to your teen's preferences and interests and assist them in discovering activities that boost their self-esteem and emotional strength. Be patient and compassionate, as growing self-esteem and emotional resilience is a continuous process that requires consistent support and encouragement. If your teen is receiving professional help, consider reviewing these activities with their therapist to ensure they correspond with their therapeutic goals.

Chapter 12

Impacts of PTSD in teens academic performance

PTSD can have major implications for a teen's academic performance due to the emotional, cognitive, and behavioral issues they may suffer as a result of their trauma. Some of the common impacts include:

Concentration Difficulties: PTSD can make it tough for teens to concentrate and focus on academic assignments. Their minds may be distracted with intrusive thoughts or memories related to the trauma.

Memory Impairment: PTSD can damage memory abilities, making it harder for kids to store and recall knowledge needed for examinations and assignments.

Decreased Motivation: Teens with PTSD may experience a lack of interest and motivation in their academics due to the emotional toll of trauma.

Absence and disinterest: PTSD symptoms, such as flashbacks or nightmares, can lead to absence from school or disinterest in classroom activities.

Emotional Distress: Intense feelings linked with PTSD, such as anxiety, melancholy, or impatience, might interfere with a teen's ability to focus on their academics.

Poor Sleep Quality: Sleep difficulties are prevalent in individuals with PTSD, resulting in weariness and poor attentiveness during school hours.

Avoidance of Triggers: Teens with PTSD may avoid circumstances or topics at school that remind them of their trauma, which can limit their involvement and engagement in learning activities.

Decline in Grades: The cumulative impact of attention issues, memory impairment, diminished motivation, and emotional suffering can contribute to a decline in academic performance.

Interpersonal Challenges: PTSD can damage kids' capacity to build and maintain healthy relationships with peers and teachers, which can impact their social experiences at school.

Inconsistent Performance: Teens with PTSD may experience changes in their academic performance. Some days, people may be able to handle it better, while other days, their symptoms may be more pronounced.

Difficulty with Organization and Time Management: PTSD can impede kids' ability to arrange their academics and manage their time properly.

Limited Future Planning: Teens with PTSD may find it tough to picture their future or set academic and career objectives owing to emotions of uncertainty and hopelessness.

It's crucial for educators and parents to be aware of these potential implications and provide appropriate assistance and accommodations for teens with PTSD. Collaborating with mental health specialists and school personnel can help establish a more understanding and accommodating atmosphere to enhance the academic performance and well-being of these kids. Encouraging open communication and obtaining professional help when needed are crucial steps in helping teens with PTSD handle their academic issues.

Chapter 13

Impacts of PTSD in relationships with family, friends and romantic partners

Post-Traumatic Stress Disorder (PTSD) can have severe implications for relationships with family, friends, and romantic partners. The symptoms of PTSD and the problems that come with them can strain these relationships in numerous ways.

FAMILY RELATIONSHIPS:

Increased Tension: PTSD symptoms such as impatience, hostility, and emotional numbing can lead to increased tension and conflicts within the family.

Communication Breakdown: Difficulties in expressing feelings and addressing traumatic experiences can result in communication breakdowns between the teen with PTSD and family members.

Role Changes: The dynamic within the family may change as the teen with PTSD may retreat or become less involved in family activities, leading to shifts in family roles.

Overprotection: Family members may become overprotective of the teen with PTSD, unwittingly limiting their independence and self-esteem.

Feeling Misunderstood: The teen with PTSD may feel misunderstood or condemned by family members who may not fully appreciate the complexity of their experiences and emotions.

FRIENDSHIPS:

Isolation: PTSD symptoms can lead to social withdrawal, prompting the teen to isolate oneself from friends and peers.

Difficulty Trusting: Teens with PTSD may find it harder to trust others, making it hard to build or sustain friendships.

Misunderstanding: Friends may fail to understand the teen's emotional reactions or reactions to triggers, leading to pressure in the friendship.

Fear of Burdening Others: Teens with PTSD may resist reaching out to peers for support, afraid that their trauma-related concerns would burden their friends.

ROMANTIC RELATIONSHIPS:

Emotional Distance: PTSD symptoms, such as emotional numbing or avoidance, can cause emotional distance between romantic partners.

Communication Challenges: Difficulty in discussing traumatic experiences or emotions might hamper open communication and emotional connection.

Triggers and memories: Romantic partners may not fully realize the impact of triggers and memories on the teen, leading to misunderstandings or dissatisfaction.

Attachment Insecurity: A kid with PTSD may struggle with attachment insecurity, leading to difficulty building and sustaining a solid link with their romantic partner.

Feeling Unsupported: If the spouse lacks awareness or comprehension of PTSD, the teen may feel unsupported on their road to healing.

It's crucial to acknowledge these potential implications and offer help and understanding to people with PTSD. Communication, empathy, and obtaining professional help, such as therapy or counseling, can play a crucial role in overcoming the issues faced by PTSD and strengthening relationships with family, friends, and love partners. It's crucial to develop an environment of patience, compassion, and non-judgment, enabling people with PTSD to feel safe and supported in their relationships.

Chapter 14

Ways to empower PTSD teens to take control of their recovery

Empowering kids with PTSD to take responsibility for their recovery can dramatically increase their healing process and promote their feelings of agency and resilience. Here are some methods to empower them:

Educate Them About PTSD: Provide age-appropriate information about PTSD and its symptoms so they understand their experiences better. Knowledge can help minimize the fear and shame associated with the disease.

Encourage Open Communication: Create a secure and non-judgmental space for your teen to communicate about their thoughts, worries, and experiences. Listen actively and validate their emotions.

Collaborate on Treatment: Involve your teen in decisions regarding their treatment plan. Let them have a say in therapy alternatives and investigate what works best for them.

Set Realistic Goals: Encourage your teen to set achievable goals for their recovery. Celebrate their progress, no matter how modest, to improve their confidence and motivation.

Teach Coping Skills: Help your teen build healthy coping techniques to manage stress and anxiety. Offer instruction on relaxation techniques, mindfulness, and other coping tactics.

Foster Self-Reflection: Encourage your teen to engage in self-reflection and journaling. Reflecting on their emotions and experiences might lead to better self-awareness and understanding.

Provide Positive Reinforcement: Offer praise and encouragement for their efforts in controlling PTSD symptoms and working towards recovery.

Promote Self-Advocacy: Encourage your teen to advocate for their needs and speak with their mental health experts about their treatment preferences and progress.

Normalize requesting Help: Let your kid know that requesting help is a show of strength, not weakness. Normalize therapy and counseling as vital resources for support and healing.

Encourage Self-Care: Promote self-care behaviors, such as regular exercise, proper sleep, and engaging in activities they enjoy, to promote their general well-being.

Involve Them in Support Groups: If suitable, involve your teen in support groups or peer networks where they can interact with others who have similar experiences. Sharing stories and support can be empowering.

Focus on qualities: Highlight your teen's qualities and talents. Building on their positive attributes can boost their self-esteem and belief in their ability to overcome obstacles.

Respect Their Boundaries: Recognize your teen's demand for personal space and privacy. Allow them to create boundaries as they feel comfortable.

Encourage Problem-Solving: Teach problem-solving skills and encourage your teen to brainstorm solutions to issues they experience.

Celebrate Resilience: Acknowledge and celebrate your teen's resilience and capacity to cope with PTSD. Recognize their fortitude in acknowledging their experience and working towards recovery.

Remember to be patient and understanding throughout the process. Empowering youth with PTSD to take ownership of their rehabilitation is about delivering direction, support, and validation as they navigate their healing journey. Encourage them to take modest steps ahead and tell them that you are there to assist them every step of the way. If needed, seek professional aid to provide further support and advice in their recovery journey.

Conclusion

In conclusion, "Parenting Teens with PTSD" discusses the specific problems and complexities experienced by parents and caregivers in assisting their adolescents on the journey to healing and recovery. Throughout this book, we have looked into the impact of PTSD on teenagers' emotional, behavioral, and academic well-being, shedding light on the significance of creating safe and non-judgmental spaces for them.

The book emphasizes the importance of empathy, understanding, and active communication in creating solid and durable relationships with PTSD-affected youth. By giving practical solutions and coping processes, we try to empower parents to negotiate the complexity of PTSD with confidence and compassion.

Our investigation of the implications of PTSD on relationships with family, friends, and romantic partners underscores the necessity of creating a supportive network for youth, helping them to feel accepted and validated in their journey to recovery.

Throughout this journey, we have realized the importance of developing self-esteem and emotional strength in teens with PTSD and encouraging them to take responsibility for their healing process. By providing youth with knowledge, coping skills, and a sense of agency, we want to impart hope and optimism for a brighter future.

As parents and caregivers, we realize the challenges that lie ahead, but we are inspired by the perseverance and fortitude of these extraordinary young beings. Together, we can create a society where teenagers with PTSD find comfort, support, and possibilities for growth.

In conclusion, "Parenting Teens with PTSD" serves as a guiding light for parents, caregivers, and professionals alike, bringing insights, practical assistance, and emotional understanding. Let us come together to create an environment of love, compassion, and empowerment, paving the way for these brave kids to triumph over their trauma and discover a future full of healing, hope, and happiness.

Printed in Great Britain
by Amazon